WHY DO MY EYES ITCH?

✦ and other questions about allergies ✦

Angela Royston

Heinemann Library
Chicago, Illinois

© 2003 Reed Educational & Professional Publishing
Published by Heinemann Library,
an imprint of Reed Educational & Professional Publishing,
Chicago, Illinois

Customer Service 888-454-2279
Visit our website at www.heinemannlibrary.com

Designed by Joanna Sapwell and StoryBooks
Illustrations by Nick Hawken
Originated by Ambassador Litho
Printed by South China Printers, Hong Kong

07 06 05 04 03
10 9 8 7 6 5 4 3 2 1

Library of Congress Cataloging-in-Publication Data
Royston, Angela.
   Why do my eyes itch? : and other questions about allergies / Angela
Royston.
      p. cm. -- (Body matters)
Summary: Answers common questions about allergies.
Includes index.
   ISBN 1-40340-207-8 (HC)   ISBN 1-40340-462-3 (PB)
   1. Allergy--Juvenile literature. [1. Allergy.] I. Title. II. Series.
   RC585 .R695 2002
   616.97--dc21
                        2002003548

Acknowledgments
The author and publishers are grateful to the following for permission to reproduce copyright material:
p. 4 P.A. Photos; pp. 5, 6, 7, 8, 9, 11, 12, 17, 23, 26, 28 Science Photo Library; p. 13 Mike Wyndham; pp. 14, 15, 20, 21, 22 Gareth Boden; p. 16 Dr. Jeremy Burgess/Science Photo Library; p. 18 Bsip; pp. 19, 27 Corbis; p. 24 Mike Bluestone/Science Photo Library; p. 25 Simon Fraser/Science Photo Library.

Cover photograph reproduced with permission of Tudor Photography.

Every effort has been made to contact copyright holders of any material reproduced in this book.
Any omissions will be rectified in subsequent printings if notice is given to the publisher.

Some words are shown in bold, **like this.** You can find out what they mean by looking in the glossary.

CONTENTS

WHAT IS AN ALLERGY?

An **allergy** occurs when the body thinks that something is harmful to it, although the same thing is harmless to most people. For example, some people are very **sensitive** to peanuts. If they eat anything with peanuts in it, their bodies treat the peanuts as harmful **germs.**

The body's defenses

The body has several ways of defending itself from things that harm it. White blood **cells** attack and destroy dirt and germs. And, when a new kind of germ enters the body, the blood makes a special kind of cell, called an **antibody,** to attack it. It makes a different antibody for each kind of germ.

This girl has severe allergies. Because she is allergic to so many things she has to live in this special tent.

Histamine

When part of the body is damaged, it releases a chemical called **histamine.** Histamine allows blood to flood the damaged area, bringing extra white blood cells and antibodies to fight any invading germs. The extra blood can also make the damaged area of the body red or swollen.

Allergic reaction

Something that causes an allergy is called an allergen. When someone is allergic to something, their blood makes antibodies against it. As soon as the antibodies detect the allergen their body releases histamine. The histamine can make them sneeze and their nose run. It may make their skin red and itchy. It can even make them vomit. Drugs called antihistamines stop histamine from working in the body. These drugs are often used to treat allergies.

COMMON CAUSES OF ALLERGIES:

- pollen
- dust mites
- feathers
- cat hair
- mold
- soap
- certain foods

This is what histamine looks like under a microscope. When you are allergic to something, your body produces too much histamine. It can affect your breathing or make you vomit.

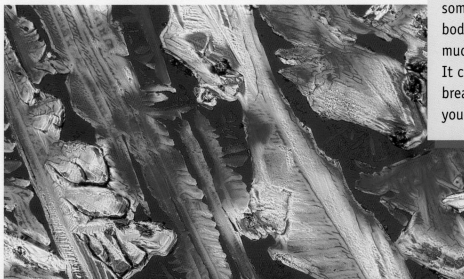

5

WHY DO MY EYES ITCH?

Your eyes itch when something irritates the inside of your eyelids. If a large speck of dust blows into your eye, your eye hurts. Smaller dust specks may make your eyes itch. Tiny specks include **germs,** cigarette smoke, and other kinds of air pollution. If you are allergic to something, such as pollen, that makes your eyes itch too.

Eye wash

A film of salty water covers each eye and helps to keep it moist and clean. Every time you blink, your eyelid washes your eye like a windshield wiper. When something irritates your eye, your body makes extra salty water to wash it out.

This boy's eyelids are red and swollen because he is allergic to pollen. Pollen makes his eyelids itch and his eyes water.

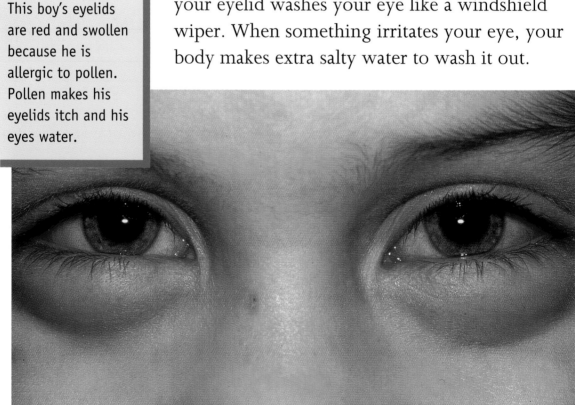

Swollen eyelids

If your eyelids are allergic to something, your body releases **histamine.** This makes your eyelids red and swollen and your eyes itchy. Taking **antihistamine** will help to reduce the effects. Infections, such as conjunctivitis, also make your eyelids red and swollen.

If you are allergic to cigarette smoke, it will make your eyes itchy and sore and will make your eyelids swell.

IRRITATING SPECKS

- Pollen is a very fine dust made by flowers.

- Germs are too small to be seen. Each kind of germ makes you ill in a different way. One germ that makes your eyes itch causes conjunctivitis.

- Millions of tiny specks of dirt float through the air. Most are too small to see. They are made by factories and cars.

- Cigarette smoke is tiny specks of burnt tobacco.

WHAT IS HAY FEVER?

Grasses have small, green flowers that produce a lot of pollen. Here, the clusters of fine, yellow dust have been magnified.

Suffering from hay fever is like having a cold for weeks on end. People with hay fever sneeze. Their noses run all the time and their eyes are red and itchy. Their faces may become puffy and they feel ill. Hay fever is caused by an **allergy** to pollen.

What is pollen?

Pollen is a fine, yellow powder that flowers produce in order to make new seeds. To make a new seed, a single grain of male pollen joins with the female sex **cell** of another flower. Some kinds of plants, such as grasses and trees, rely on the wind to blow their pollen from one flower to another. In this process the grains of pollen float far and wide.

Pollen count

In early summer, weather reports often give a pollen count as a figure out of ten. The higher the figure, the more pollen there is in the air. Different plants produce pollen at particular times of the spring and summer, but most produce it in late spring and early summer.

Trapped indoors

People who suffer from hay fever try to avoid going near grass and flowers when the pollen count is high. This means that they have to keep out of their yards in early summer. Many hay fever sufferers also take **antihistamine** to reduce their symptoms.

This girl suffers from hay fever. When she breathes pollen in the air into her nose, it makes her sneeze.

HOW DO ALLERGIES AFFECT BREATHING?

Feathers, wool, pet hairs, dust, and dust mites all produce fine grains or powders. Like pollen, the fine grains float in the air and can cause **allergies** that affect breathing.

An allergy can affect any part of the body that the air you breathe in reaches—including the nose and the bronchial tubes.

What happens to the air you breathe in?

When you breathe in, air passes through your nose and mouth into the **bronchial tubes** and then to thinner tubes in your lungs. All of these breathing tubes are lined with fine hairs and **mucus** to catch any dirt, **germs,** or dust that you breathe in with the air. Inside your lungs, oxygen from the air passes into the blood, and waste carbon dioxide (gas in the air) leaves the blood to join the air that is breathed out.

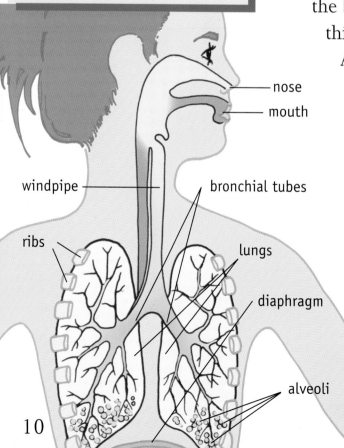

nose

mouth

windpipe

bronchial tubes

ribs

lungs

diaphragm

alveoli

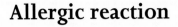

Allergic reaction

People often sneeze or cough when they breathe in an **allergen.** This is the body's way of getting rid of dust in the nose or throat. The nose also produces extra mucus to help wash the allergen away. Some people only react to an allergen when it reaches their lungs. Then the body produces **histamine** that makes the bronchial tubes become narrower and even close up. This can make it difficult to breathe in and out.

Pets make some people sneeze or cough. Cats that have fleas and dandruff are more likely to cause allergies.

Asthma

People who have **asthma** also find it difficult to breathe. During an asthma attack, their bronchial tubes become tight and they make a wheezing sound as they breathe. An attack may last a few minutes or much longer. An allergy is a common cause of an asthma attack, although there are many other causes, too.

Avoiding allergens

Some **allergens** are easier to avoid than others. If you are allergic to feathers, then you can use a pillow and comforter made of **synthetic materials.** If you are allergic to wool, then you can wear clothes made of cotton or synthetic fabrics. And if you are allergic to cats or dogs, then you should not keep them as pets.

Avoiding dust and dust mites

Dust is harder to avoid. Most of the dust in your home is made of tiny flakes of dead skin. If you are allergic to dust, it is helpful to vacuum all the

Dust mites are tiny insects that are too small to see without a microscope. This is what a dust mite looks like when it is magnified.

floors and clean your bedding every day. Dust mites feed on dust. They are so small they pass straight through most vacuum cleaners. Some cleaners have a special filter for catching tiny grains of dust and dust mites. Carpets collect dust, so you may have to do without them.

Antihistamine

Antihistamines are drugs that reduce the symptoms of an **allergy**, but they are not a cure. When antihistamine tablets are taken regularly, they work for a long period of time. Antihistamine can also be sprayed or dropped directly into the nose. This gives quick relief for a short time, but can damage the delicate lining inside the nose if used over many years.

This girl is using an inhaler that contains an antihistamine because she is very allergic to dust. The antihistamine reduces the symptoms of the allergy.

ALLERGY SUFFERERS

About one in every five people in the United States suffers from an allergy.

13

WHY DOES MY SKIN ITCH?

Some **allergies** affect the skin. If you have **sensitive** skin, **biological detergents** and scented soaps and cosmetics may make your skin itch. People with sensitive skin may have to buy pure soap, non-biological soap, and non-allergenic cosmetics.

Sun allergy

Some people are allergic to the Sun. Their skin breaks out in small blisters unless they wear long-sleeved shirts and pants and avoid strong sunshine. Everyone should protect their skin against damage from the Sun's rays by wearing a shirt and sun hat and rubbing suntan lotion into their skin.

People with sensitive skin have to be careful which detergent they use to wash their clothes and which soaps and creams they use on their skin.

Food allergies

Many people are allergic to strawberries, nuts, or other foods. If they eat something with nuts in it, for example, their skin may become red and blotchy. Their skin feels very uncomfortable for a few hours until the allergy dies down.

Other itchy things

Having itchy skin does not mean that you have an allergy. Many people find that rough cloth or fluffy wool, such as mohair, feels itchy against their skin. Most rashes, such as heat rash and the rash caused by chickenpox, are itchy too. Dabbing on camomile lotion or a solution of sodium bicarbonate on your skin helps to soothe the itching.

Try not to scratch if you have a condition such as chicken pox, eczema, or an allergy. Scratching may make your skin red and sore.

THINGS THAT CAN MAKE YOUR SKIN ITCH

Many different things can cause skin allergies if you are allergic to them. They include:

- soap and detergents
- eating strawberries, shellfish, eggs, milk, nuts
- insect bites and stings
- eczema
- medicines such as aspirin and penicillin
- stinging nettles

Stings and bites

When an insect such as a bee or wasp stings you, it injects poison into your blood. Your body's natural defense to a sting is to produce **histamine.** Histamine makes the skin around the sting swell up and become red and itchy.

Insect bites

Some insects, such as mosquitoes and head lice, bite animals and people in order to feed on their blood. As a mosquito stabs your skin with its mouth, some of its saliva runs into the wound. The saliva stops your blood from clotting so that the mosquito can suck up more blood. But most people are allergic to the mosquito's saliva. Their body produces histamine and it makes the bite red and itchy.

When a bee stings you, it often leaves its stinger in your skin. Pull the stinger out very carefully.

Treating insect stings and bites

Antihistamine cream helps to stop stings and bites from hurting and itching. But if you have caught head lice, the only way to stop your scalp from itching is to get rid of the lice. To do this you need to use a special shampoo or lotion that you can buy at the pharmacy. Scabies is a very itchy skin condition. It is caused by a tiny mite that burrows beneath the skin. It needs to be treated by a doctor.

Extreme shock

A few people are so allergic to insect bites their bodies go into **extreme shock.** If this happens, get medical help at once.

STINGING INSECTS
bees, wasps, hornets, ants

BITING INSECTS
mosquitoes, gnats, fleas, head lice

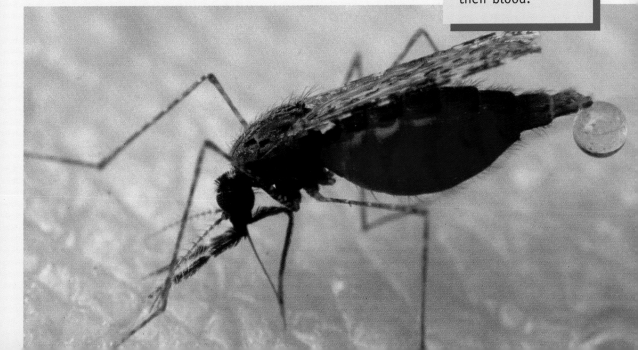

This is a mosquito. Mosquitoes bite people and animals to feed on their blood.

CAN YOU CATCH ECZEMA?

Eczema is a condition that makes the skin dry, swollen, and itchy. Sometimes little blisters form on the skin. They may become crusty when they burst. Eczema may occur on any part of the body, but is common on the elbows and behind the knees. There are several kinds of eczema, but none of them are catching. One kind tends to run in families. It is common among young children, but they have often grown out of it by the time they are four years old.

This boy has eczema on the back of his knees. It is important not to scratch eczema, because scratching makes it worse.

Allergic eczema

Another kind of eczema is caused by an allergic reaction to something the person touches. This is called contact eczema. Different things cause contact eczema in different people. It is often triggered by plants, cosmetics, medicines, and foods that include wheat and milk. People who have allergic eczema often suffer from hay fever or **asthma** too.

Allergies from work

Some people are allergic to chemicals and other things that they touch at work. Some photographers, for example, are allergic to the chemicals that are used to develop photographs. Some bakers and grocers are allergic to foods that they have to touch, and people who work with tar may be allergic to it.

Treating allergic eczema

The best way to treat allergic eczema is to try to avoid the things that trigger it. Using special oils to clean the skin is more soothing than using soap and water. Special creams can also help to reduce the swelling and itching.

Some people find that swimming in the ocean can help to reduce eczema. Sunshine can trigger eczema but it usually makes it better.

19

WHY DO PEANUTS MAKE SOME PEOPLE SICK?

This girl has just eaten some nuts by mistake and is feeling very sick. People who are allergic to nuts often react to them very quickly.

Many people are allergic to peanuts or other nuts, such as pecans and walnuts. Eating even a small amount of peanuts can make them vomit. Vomiting is the body's way of getting rid of something poisonous that you have eaten. So if someone is allergic to nuts, their body reacts as if the nuts are poisonous.

Avoiding nuts

Some people are allergic to just one or two foods. Other people are allergic to many. Avoiding certain foods, such as nuts, is not as easy as it sounds. Many kinds of foods, including many cereals, contain small amounts of nuts.

Some people are extremely **sensitive** to even tiny amounts of a particular food. The fact that a machine in a factory previously processed nuts is enough to trigger the **allergy.** That is why many products say "may contain traces of nuts" on the label.

Other symptoms of food allergy

If you eat something that you are allergic to, your mouth may tingle and your lips, tongue, and throat may swell up and go numb. It may also give you stomach ache and diarrhea. Some people are so allergic to nuts or other food, their bodies can go into **extreme shock** if they eat them. People who are likely to react like this usually carry medicine that will help them to recover quickly.

If you are allergic to nuts or any other kind of food, you have to check the ingredients on food labels before you eat anything.

Skin reaction

Food **allergies** do not affect only the **digestive system.** The most common sign of a food allergy is an itchy rash. Many people who are allergic to strawberries, shellfish, and nuts break out in a rash or in red blotches when they eat them. A food allergy can also make it difficult for some people to breathe.

This girl cannot eat anything that has cheese in it. Cheese makes her irritable and keeps her from sleeping.

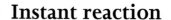

Instant reaction

Many people react very quickly to a food they are allergic to. Within minutes their skin breaks out in a rash, or they feel sick, or their mouth swells up. If this happens, it is fairly easy to tell what has caused the reaction. Other people take longer to react. If you are sick three days after eating something, you may not realize the cause.

Food can affect other conditions

A food allergy may trigger **eczema,** an **asthma** attack, or other conditions, such as migraines. A migraine is a bad headache that may cause people to vomit or feel dizzy. They may see wiggly lines or dots in front of their eyes. Different things cause migraines in different people, but many migraine sufferers find that eating cheese, or chocolate, or a chemical called monosodium glutamate triggers a migraine attack.

COMMON FOOD ALLERGIES:

- peanuts and other nuts
- strawberries, tomatoes
- milk, cheese, yogurt
- chocolate
- wheat
- fish or shellfish
- pork
- monosodium glutamate (used in potato chips, Chinese food, and other foods)
- medicines such as penicillin and aspirin

Eating strawberries, shellfish, or other foods can cause a rash like this. It may only last a few hours but it is very uncomfortable.

CAN FOOD ALLERGIES BE CURED?

An **allergy** cannot be cured, but it can go away. Many young children grow out of allergies. If you are allergic to cheese, for example, the allergy may disappear when you are older. Or, if you avoid eating cheese for several months, your body may become less **sensitive** to cheese. If you have one or more allergies, there are several things you can do to reduce their effect.

Avoiding allergens

If you are allergic to something, it is best to avoid it. This is not always easy. If you are allergic to wheat, for example, you have to read the labels of cookies and other foods before you can eat them. When you are eating out, you often have to ask whether the food you want to eat includes something you are allergic to. However hard they try, most

This girl is taking a drug that includes **antihistamine.** It will allow her to eat some foods she is allergic to.

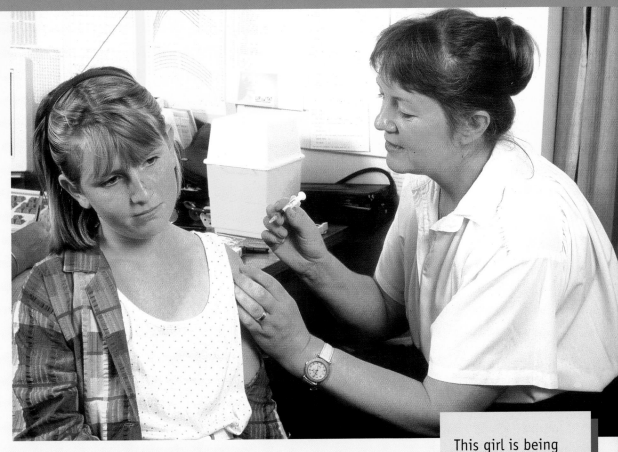

This girl is being injected with a tiny amount of the food she is allergic to. As the dose is increased, her body becomes used to the food and no longer reacts to it.

people who are allergic to some kind of food eat it by mistake from time to time.

A little at a time

Some people who are allergic to foods can eat them, as long as they do not eat too much of them too often. A few people become allergic to more and more different foods. They have to be very careful. They eat a few kinds of food for four or five days, and then they eat different foods for the next four or five days. In this way, they hope that their bodies will accept the foods.

HOW DO DOCTORS TEST FOR ALLERGIES?

It is sometimes difficult to figure out what is causing an **allergy.** You may be able to detect the what is responsible yourself or you may need the help of an allergy clinic.

Detecting the allergen

If your skin suddenly develops an allergic rash, try to remember whether you recently used a new cream or soap. Some allergies develop slowly, so an old cream could be the cause. If you cannot find the **allergen,** stop using everything that it could be. If the rash goes away, then start using the creams again, but reintroduce them one at a time. You should then discover the allergen. Doctors sometimes use the same method to detect the cause of food allergies.

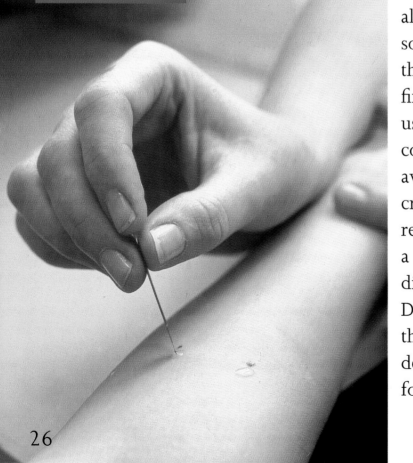

This girl is being given a test to find out what she is allergic to. She may be allergic to more than one allergen.

26

Skin prick test

If you are allergic to something that affects your breathing system, an allergy clinic may use a skin prick test to find out what the allergens are. Tiny amounts of different allergens are dropped onto your skin. You are allergic to any allergens that make your skin react.

Blood test

Sometimes the clinic can find the allergens by testing a small sample of your blood. They look for particular **antibodies** in the blood. If you are allergic to pollen, for example, your blood will have antibodies against it.

Being allergic is often inherited, but the allergy itself is not. Each member of this family suffers from a different allergy.

Inheriting allergies

Allergies often run in families. If one parent has an allergy, then one child out of three will probably have an allergy too. If both parents have allergies, then two or even three children out of three will probably have an allergy.

ARE ALLERGIES DANGEROUS?

Most allergies are not dangerous, but if an allergy leads to **extreme shock** then it is dangerous. Extreme shock is also called anaphylactic shock. It can happen very quickly and involves the whole body.

Extreme shock

The person's lips, tongue, and face swell up and they sometimes look very pale. They find it difficult to breathe and become unconscious. The person's blood pressure becomes very low. If they do not receive medical help at once, they will die. A doctor can inject drugs to reduce the person's swelling and increase their blood pressure. Oxygen helps them to breathe normally. The most common causes of extreme shock are bee and wasp stings, nuts, shellfish, eggs, and antibiotics.

This woman is enjoying seafood with her meal. If she is allergic to shellfish, she should not risk eating it because shellfish can cause extreme shock.

BODY MAP

Mucus washes dirt, germs, and allergens from the nose

Tears wash dirt and other irritants from the eye

Saliva helps to kill some germs

Fine hairs and mucus push dirt, germs, and allergens from breathing tubes

Stomach muscles push out poisonous food and allergens when you vomit

White cells and antibodies in the blood kill germs

Histamine allows blood to flood damaged areas of the body

GLOSSARY

allergen something that causes an allergy

allergy when the body reacts to something as though it were a germ, although the same thing is harmless to most people

antibodies special cells carried in the blood that attack particular germs or allergens

antihistamine medicine that blocks the effects of histamine

asthma condition in which the breathing tubes become narrow, making it difficult to breathe

biological detergents soap and liquids that can contain enzymes (special chemicals) that remove dirt from clothes

bronchial tubes tubes that carry air in and out of the lungs

cell smallest building block of living things. The body has many kinds of cells, including lung cells and skin cells.

digestive system parts of the body involved with digesting food

eczema condition that causes dry, itchy skin, sometimes with small blisters

extreme shock life-threatening reaction to an allergen

germs tiny living things that can make you sick

histamine chemical made by the body when part of the body is damaged or when antibodies detect a germ or allergen

mucus slime that coats the inside of parts of the body, including the nose and bronchial tubes

sensitive easily affected by something

synthetic materials materials, such as plastic, nylon, and polyester, that are made from oil

FURTHER READING

Monroe, Judy. *Allergies*. Minnetonka, Minn.: Capstone Press, 2001.

Silverstein, Alvin. *Allergies*. Danbury, Conn.: Franklin Watts, 2000.

Weitzman, Elizabeth. *Let's Talk about Having Allergies*. New York: PowerKids Press, 1997.

INDEX

Embossing an envelope

You could emboss your initials on the cover of a small book. (See pages 24-25 for instructions on how to make a book.)

Use paper clips to attach an envelope to your cardboard cut-out. Make sure that your initials will be the right way up when the envelope is sealed. Use the teaspoon to smooth the flap into the cut-out letters as you did for the writing paper.

Patterns

As well as letters, you can also emboss patterns. Use simple shapes as they are easiest to cut out.

Cards and envelopes

You will need:

Thick, bright paper
Calligraphy pens
Tracing paper
Scissors and a craft knife
Glue
A ruler
Parcel ribbon

Tree card

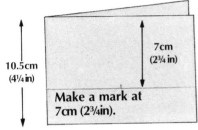

7cm
(2¾ in)

10.5cm
(4¼ in)

**Make a mark at
7cm (2¾in).**

1. Cut a piece of paper that measures 10.5 x 28cm (4¼ x 11in). Fold it in half. Draw a faint line 7cm (2¾in) from the top.

To transfer your lettering to the card see page 30.

2. On tracing paper, draw around the front and draw in the faint line. Write your message along the line and on the pot and trunk.

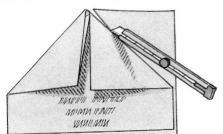

3. Fold the top two corners in so they meet in the middle at the mark on the line. Cut off the top layer of the right-hand flap.

The pattern on the tied card was drawn with a pen and gouache paint (available from an art suppliers).

The hearts on the tree card were drawn with a calligraphy pen.

The lines on the striped, zigzag card were painted in ink using a homemade felt-tip pen (see page 11).

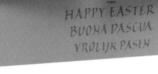

HAPPY EASTER
BUONA PASCUA
VROLIJK PASEN

Félicitatio
tulacje·Gr
ations·Féli
rd·Gratulo
gratul

GROSSES BI
WITH LO
TANTI BA

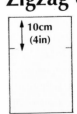

4. You could use a calligraphy pen to draw a pattern on the flaps, or print a design with a rubber stamp (see pages 10 -11).

Zigzag card

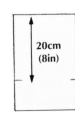

10cm
(4in)

Turn the paper over.

20cm
(8in)

1. Cut a piece of paper 20 x 30cm (8 x 12in). Make pencil marks at 10cm (4in) on one side and 20cm (8in) on the other side.

Tied card

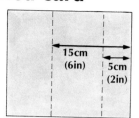

1. Cut a piece of bright paper 24 x 20cm (9½ x 8in). Mark and score lines 5cm (2in) and 15cm (6in) from the right-hand side.

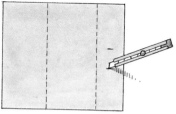

2. Use a craft knife to make two slits, 1cm (½ in) long on the narrow section, 8cm (3in) in from each end.

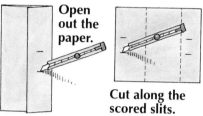

Open out the paper.

Cut along the scored slits.

3. Fold in the flaps, with the narrow one on top. Slide the craft knife through each slit to score lines on the layer below.

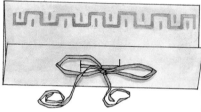

4. Decorate the front and the inside of the card. Thread a piece of parcel ribbon through both sets of slits and tie a bow.

Envelopes

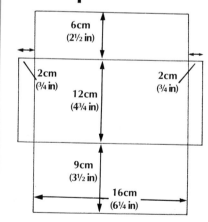

6cm (2½ in)

2cm (¾ in)

12cm (4¾ in)

2cm (¾ in)

9cm (3½ in)

16cm (6¼ in)

The tree card will fit in this size.

1. Copy the measurements above onto paper using a ruler and pencil. If you want to make an envelope for the other cards, change the width of the large rectangle from 16cm (6¼in) to 21cm (8½in).

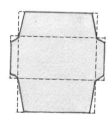

Cut around the outline shown in red.

2. Mark points 1cm (½in) from each corner. Join these points to the corners of the middle rectangle.

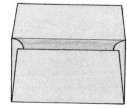

To seal the envelope, stick the top flap with a little glue.

3. Score lightly along each line and fold in the sides. Fold up the bottom. Stick this to the sides with some glue.

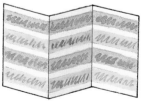

Decorate the front and write your message on the back.

2. Lightly score the paper along the marks you have made. Fold it first one way and then the other to make a zigzag.

A concertina birthday book

You will need:

2 pieces of stiff cardboard
10 x 17cm (4 x 6¾in)
A sheet of paper 56 x 15cm
(22 x 6in) for the pages
2 pieces of giftwrap 14 x 21cm
(5½ x 8½ in)
4 pieces of 25cm (10in) ribbon
A glue stick
A calligraphy pen
A ruler and a craft knife

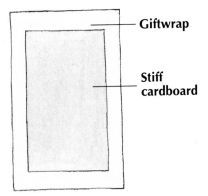

Giftwrap

Stiff cardboard

1. To make the two covers, cut the cardboard and giftwrap to the correct sizes, using a craft knife and ruler. Glue the cardboard in the middle of the giftwrap, leaving equal margins all around.

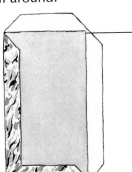

Leave a small gap at the corners.

2. Use scissors to trim the corners off the giftwrap, close to, but not touching the corners of the cardboard. Fold the giftwrap over the edges and glue them down carefully.

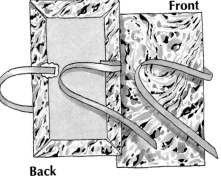

Front

Back

3. Use glue to stick the ribbons onto the inside of each cover. Make sure there is an equal amount of ribbon at each side. Trim each end diagonally to stop the ribbons from fraying.

Fold the paper into a concertina.

4. Make faint pencil marks every 8cm (3in) at the top and bottom edges of the long strip of paper. Neatly score and fold the paper one way and then the other at each set of marks (see page 31).

MAYO

JUNI

MAGGIO

JUNIO

You could decorate the covers with lettering or embossing (see pages 4-5), rather than using giftwrap.

Lettering Styles

You could use a single large letter instead of the whole word for each month. Decorate the inside of the letter with ink or paint in a contrasting shade.

The first page will be January, the sixth will be June. Leave the seventh page blank.

5. Rule double lines along the top for the name of each month. The distance between the lines depends on the size of your nib (see page 30). Write the names of the months between the lines.

6. Measure out the same lines on the other side. The lettering for July will be on page 8 and so on. December will be on page 13. Leave page 14 blank as this will be stuck to a cover.

7. When you have finished lettering both sides, use glue to stick page 14 in the middle of the front cover. Glue page 7 onto the back cover. Tie the ribbons to close the book.

Giftwrap and tags

Y ou can use calligraphy to decorate large sheets of paper, such as brown parcel paper. You could also experiment with giftwrap that has a simple pattern on it. Before you start, calculate roughly how much paper you will need to wrap your present.

Gold ink used with a homemade pen (see right)

Rubber stamps

You will need:

A large eraser
A craft knife
Tracing paper
A soft and a hard pencil
Double pencils (see page 3) or a calligraphy pen
A large sheet of paper
An ink pad from a stationer's

Brown parcel paper printed with a rubber stamp

1. Draw around the eraser onto the tracing paper. Draw a letter or shape inside the outline, using the pencils or a pen.

Use some of your giftwrap to make a matching tag.

Stripes drawn with a felt-tip pen and a cotton-tipped stick, then printed with a rubber stamp

2. Turn the tracing paper over, place it on the eraser. Use a hard pencil to transfer the lettering to the eraser (see page 30).

3. Put the eraser on a cutting surface (see page 31). Carefully cut around the outline of the letter or shape using a craft knife.

Keep your fingers away from the blade.

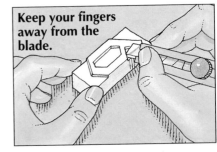

4. Carefully slice away the area around the letter, so that the letter stands about 2mm ($^1/_{16}$in) above the surface of the eraser.

Homemade pens

You will need:

A craft knife
Thick cardboard
Plastic food wrap
Felt
A rubber band
2 cotton-tipped sticks
Ink or paint

Plastic food wrap

Felt

Cut the cardboard into a strip 15 x 2cm (6 x ¾in). Wrap some food wrap around one end of it. Cut a strip of felt the same width as the cardboard. Secure it over the end of the cardboard with a rubber band. Dip the pen into ink or paint and write with it. For smaller letters, cut a narrower strip.

You can also make a double-nibbed pen using the same method. Once you have secured the food wrap and the felt, cut a V-shape into the end of the pen, through the layers.

Use a cotton-tipped stick as a pen, or tape two together to make a thicker pen. Try using this with ink instead of using a felt-tip pen.

Fluid writing

Another technique is to use artists' masking fluid from an art supplier's, with a homemade pen (see right).

Paint the fluid onto paper. When it is dry, sponge ink over it and leave it to dry.

Gently rub the surface of the masking fluid with your finger or an eraser to reveal your lettering.

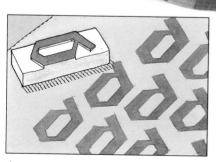

5. Press the rubber stamp onto the ink pad. Try out various repeated patterns before printing onto your large piece of paper.

An interlocking gift box

You will need:

2 sheets of cardboard, about the thickness of a cereal box, in contrasting shades
A craft knife and scissors
Glue
Tracing paper
Calligraphy pen or a broad-edge brush and paint
A ruler
An eraser

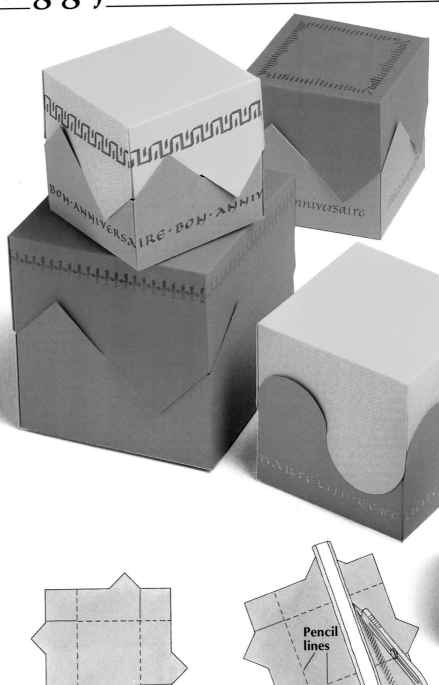

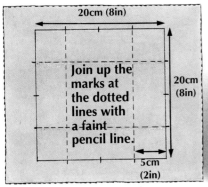

1. To make a box measuring 10 x10cm (4 x 4in), start by drawing a 20 x 20cm (8 x 8in) square on both pieces of cardboard. Measure and mark points lightly in pencil every 5cm (2in) along each side.

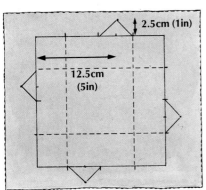

2. Mark 12.5cm (5in) along each side on both squares. Draw a dot 2.5cm (1in) above each of these marks. Join each dot to the marks on the square either side of it.

3. Using a craft knife and a ruler, carefully cut out the two halves of the box along the outlines. Also cut along the red lines indicated in the picture.

4. Gently score along all the dotted lines shown above with a craft knife (see page 31). Remove all your pencil lines from each box with an eraser.

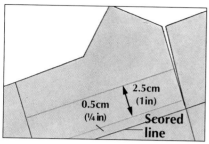

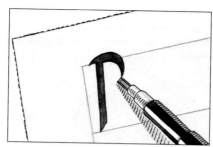

5. Decorate your box before you stick it together. Draw two faint pencil lines 0.5cm (¼in) and 2.5cm (1in) from the scored lines, as guidelines for the letters.

To make a box with wavy edges, open a pair of compasses to 2.5cm (1in) and draw a semicircle at the 12.5cm (5in) mark (see stage 2).

6. Trace over the guidelines onto a piece of tracing paper. Use the guidelines to help with the sizing and spacing of your lettering (see page 30).

7. Transfer the lettering to the side or top of the lid (see page 30). Use either a pen or a broad-edge brush and paint for the lettering.

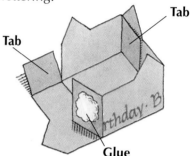

8. Fold up the edges and bend each tab at right angles to the fold. Glue the tabs inside.

9. Finally, interlock the two halves, making sure that all the triangles are on the outside.

Different-sized boxes

To make a box of a different size, draw a square with sides twice as long as you want them to be when the box is complete. To find out the distance between the marks in step 1, divide the length of the side by four. The height of the points in step 2 is half the distance between these marks.

Mugs and a bowl

You will need :

A plain china mug
Ceramic paint which hardens in an oven (available in craft shops)
Tracing paper
Clear book-covering film
A craft knife and scissors
An old toothbrush
Double pencils (see page 3)
Paper towels
A ballpoint pen
A small, clean plastic container
Old newspapers
A black felt-tip pen
Masking tape

You could save the letters you cut out at step 4 and use them to decorate a matching plate (see pages 22-23).

Remember to harden the paint on your finished object by following the paint maker's instructions.

Add simple decorations, such as dots or flowers between the letters.

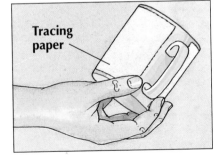

Tracing paper

1. Cut a strip of tracing paper about the same height as your mug and long enough to fit around it.

Make the thinnest part of the letters 3mm (1/8 in) wide.

2. Using double pencils, write a message or a name to fit on the tracing paper. Outline the letters with a black felt-tip pen.

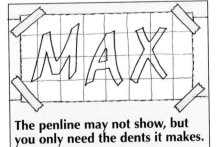

The penline may not show, but you only need the dents it makes.

3. Cut some film to fit over the tracing paper. Tape it, shiny side upward, over the letters. Trace around them with a ballpoint pen.

Stick in any middle pieces.

Cut-out area

Film

4. Place the film on a cutting surface. Use a craft knife to cut out the letters. Keep any middle pieces from the letters as you will need to stick them on the mug.

5. It is easier to stick the film onto the mug if you cut the film into smaller pieces before peeling off the backing paper. Be careful not to cut the letters.

6. Completely cover the rest of the mug, including the handle with pieces of tape. Put lots of paper towels inside the mug so that it is kept clean.

7. In the plastic container, mix a little ceramic paint with water until it is like thin cream. Cover an area with newspaper and put your mug in the middle of it.

8. To spray the letters, dip the toothbrush into the paint and hold it near the mug. Flick your fingernail along the bristles until the letter spaces are covered.

9. You could add another shade of paint once the first has dried. When all the paint is dry, peel off the film. Follow the maker's instructions to harden the paint.

Decorating a bowl

You can use exactly the same technique to decorate the outside of a bowl. To calculate the length of your message, cut a strip of tracing paper long enough to fit around the outside of the bowl.

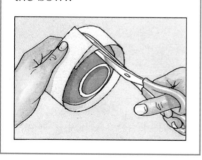

More mugs

Buy a mug with stripes on it. Draw parallel lines, the same width as the stripes. Draw a pattern between the lines then trace it onto the film.

Draw a simple calligraphy pattern (see page 19) and spray it around the base of the mug. Add small dots in a different shade with a fine paintbrush.

Buy a mug with a simple design on it. Trace the shapes onto tracing paper and add letters to fill the spaces. Try putting the letters at at different angles.

Angel decorations and cards

You will need:

Thick white paper 25 x 25cm
(10 x 10in)
A pair of compasses
A pencil and a ruler
Calligraphy pens
A small piece of gold paper
Tracing paper
A needle and thread
A craft knife and scissors

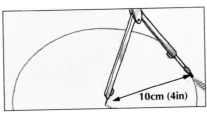

1. Open your compasses to 10cm (4in) and draw a circle on the white paper. The diameter of your circle should be 20cm (8in).

Join the marks to the central point.

2. Divide the circle into quarters with faint lines. Mark points on the outside of the circle 8mm (³⁄₈in) below the horizontal line.

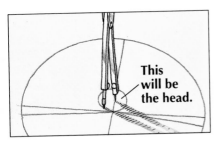

This will be the head.

3. Open the compasses to 1.5cm (⁵⁄₈in). Starting with the pencil lead on the central point, draw a circle above the horizontal line.

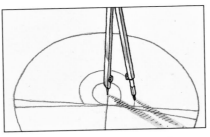

4. Open the compasses to 3cm (1¹⁄₈in) and with the point in the same place, draw an arc between the two sloping lines.

You could make several angels and hang them from different lengths of thread.

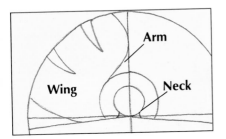

Arm

Wing

Neck

5. Draw the shapes for the wings, neck and arms on one side of the circle as shown on the diagram above.

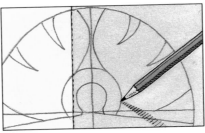

6. Trace around the shapes, turn the paper over and transfer the shapes to the other side of the circle (see page 30).

Transfer the lettering onto the angel.

Buon Natale

7. Trace around the skirt. Write a message which fits in the middle 6cm (2½in) of the skirt, so it can be read when the angel is folded.

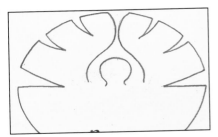

8. Cut along all the lines shown in red with a craft knife or scissors. Remove all the pencil lines with an eraser.

Assembling the angel

Fold the wings and the arms forward and roll the arms around a pencil to curl them.

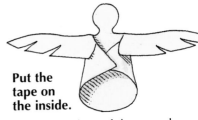

Put the tape on the inside.

Bend the skirt of the angel around to make a cone shape and stick it together with tape.

The angel as a card

To use the angel as a Christmas card, follow steps 1 to 8. Don't forget to include a halo. Either buy an envelope at least 21 x 21cm (8½ x 8½in) to fit the card, or make one following the instructions on page 7, adjusting the measurements so that the middle rectangle becomes a square measuring 21 x 21cm (8½ x 8½in) and the right one measures 21 x 18cm (8½ x 7in).

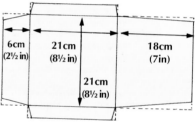

6cm (2½ in)	21cm (8½ in)	18cm (7in)
	21cm (8½ in)	

Copy the instructions from the box (below left) on how to assemble the angel. Send them in the envelope with your card.

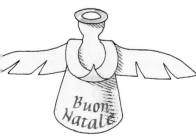

Draw a small circle with a tab on gold paper for the halo. Stick it onto the angel's head.

To make a hanging decoration, push a needle with thread through the top of the angel's head and tie the ends to make a loop.

Decorating a terracotta pot

You will need:

A clean terracotta plant pot
Tracing paper and masking tape
A broad-edge (one-stroke) paint
brush from an art supplier's
Artist's acrylic paints
A plastic lid
Carbon paper (see page 30)
Double pencils (see page 3)
Scrap paper

**Instead of drawing a pattern,
you could write a name
around the pot, or combine
lettering and patterns.**

Leave your pot on a pile of old newspapers to dry out.

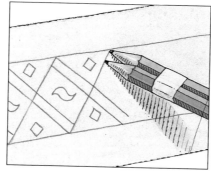

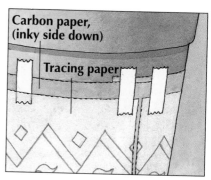

Carbon paper, (inky side down)

Tracing paper

1. Make sure the surface of the terracotta pot is absolutely clean. If you need to wash it, leave it overnight to dry out as this type of pot absorbs a lot of water.

2. To calculate the length of your decoration, cut a strip of tracing paper which fits around your pot. On scrap paper, try out different patterns using double pencils or copy some from below.

3. Once you are happy with your design, trace it onto the strip of tracing paper. Stick a piece of carbon paper onto the pot, inky side down, then tape the tracing paper over it.

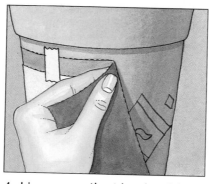

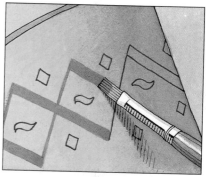

4. Use a pencil with a hard lead to trace over the outline of your pattern (see page 30). Check that it has traced completely before pulling off the papers.

5. On a lid, mix some acrylic paint with water so that it is like thin cream. Paint over the pattern with the brush. Some shades may need two coats of paint.

Depending on the shape of your pot, you could paint your decoration or lettering around the rim or the base of the pot, or both.

Calligraphic patterns

A sun clock

This clock could be hung on a wall by attaching some string to the back with masking tape.

When Roman numerals are used for the numbers on a clockface, number 4 is often shown as IIII, rather than IV. This is to balance with VIII on the opposite side.

You will need:

A clock mechanism (from a craft shop or buy a cheap clock and take it apart)
A piece of thick cardboard
A pair of compasses
Thick, bright paper in blue, orange and two shades of yellow
Calligraphy pens
Tracing paper
A pencil and a ruler
A craft knife and scissors
Masking tape
PVA (household) glue

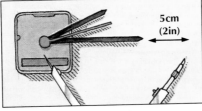

1. Open the compasses so that they are 5cm (2in) wider than the long hand of the clock. Draw a circle on the thick cardboard. Cut it out using a craft knife.

5cm (2in)

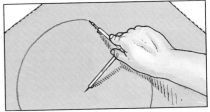

2. Draw a circle the same size as the cardboard on the dark yellow paper and on a piece of tracing paper. Use scissors to cut both of them out.

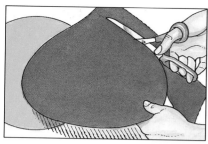

3. Reduce the width of the compasses by 8mm (³/₈in) and draw a circle on the blue paper. Cut it out, using scissors.

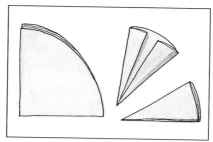

4. Fold the tracing paper into quarters. Then fold it into thirds by bending both edges in so that they overlap. Crease the folds.

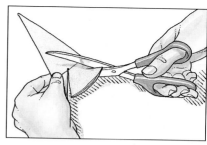

5. Draw a line 4cm (1½in) from the edge of the circle. Make a mark halfway along this line. Cut in from both corners to this mark.

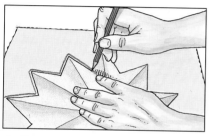

6. Open out the tracing paper and spread it out on the pale yellow paper. Draw around it, then use a ruler to straighten the lines. Cut out the star shape.

7. Set the compasses to 1cm (½in) wider than the short hand. Draw a circle on the dark yellow paper. Cut it out and put it in the middle of the star. Draw around it.

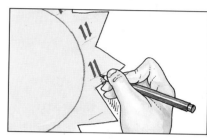

8. Each number fits on one of the points. Either draw them freehand, or try them out on tracing paper and then transfer them to the clock (see page 30).

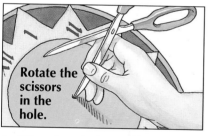

Rotate the scissors in the hole.

9. Glue the circles and the star to the cardboard, starting with the biggest one. Decorate the face (see below). Enlarge the central hole with some scissors.

10. Take the hands off the clock mechanism. Push the spindle of the mechanism through the hole from the back. Replace the hands on the front of the clock.

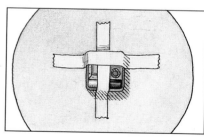

11. Attach the mechanism to the back of the clock with masking tape. If you want to make your clock more durable, paint it with a couple of coats of the glue.

Decorating the face

Make the face after attaching the circles and star in step 9. Begin by cutting an orange circle, the same size as the dark yellow one.

1. Draw in the features marked by the blue line. Cut them out carefully.

2. Glue the main part of the face and the left eye onto the yellow circle.

3. Turn over the pieces for the lips and cheek, and glue them in place.

Calligraphy on a plate

You will need:

A plain china plate
Ceramic paint which hardens in an oven (from a craft shop)
A pair of compasses
Tracing paper
A ballpoint pen
A black felt-tip pen
Double pencils (see page 3)
Scissors and a craft knife
A sponge
An old plastic lid or paper plate
Old newspapers
Book-covering film

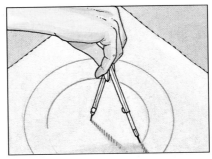

1. Draw around the china plate onto tracing paper. Draw in the rim of the plate by opening the compasses to half the width of the central area of the plate. Cut around the outline of the plate.

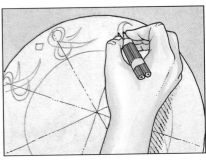

2. Fold the tracing paper into quarters and then in half again. Open it out. Using the creases as a guide for spacing, draw a pattern or lettering around the rim with double pencils.

To fill the inside shape of each bird, trace its outline onto tracing paper and cut it out. Place the tracing paper stencil on the plate and sponge through it.

The letter H was painted with a broad-edge brush.

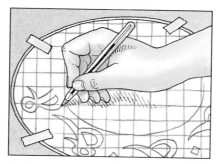

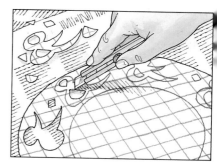

3. On the tracing paper, draw carefully around your pencil lines with a black felt-tip pen. Make any of the thin parts of your pattern or lettering at least 3mm (1/8in) wide.

4. Draw around the plate on some book-covering film. Cut it out, then tape it over the tracing paper. Trace over your design using a ballpoint pen. Also draw the inner circle on the film.

5. Place the book-covering film on a cutting surface (see page 31). Use a craft knife to cut out around the black lines that form your pattern or lettering. Keep all the shapes you have cut out.

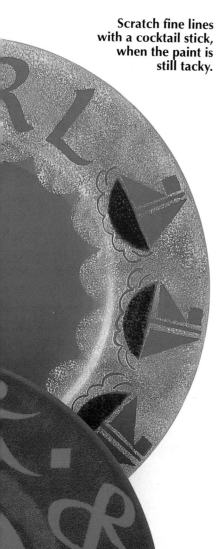

Scratch fine lines with a cocktail stick, when the paint is still tacky.

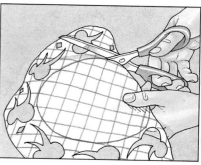

Use a felt-tip pen to make the marks.

6. Place your tracing paper over the plate and make a tiny mark at each crease. One by one, peel the backing paper off each shape and stick it onto the rim, using the marks as a guide.

7. Use scissors to cut out the central circle from the book-covering film. Peel the backing paper off the circle and stick it very carefully in the middle of the plate.

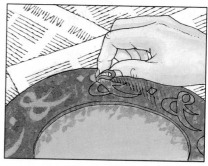

8. Put a little ceramic paint on the plastic lid. Dip the sponge into it and dab it onto some newspaper to get rid of excess paint. Dab the sponge lightly all over the rim of the plate.

9. When the paint is still tacky, carefully peel off the film. It may help to slip the blade of a craft knife under it to start it off. Follow the maker's instructions for hardening the paint.

An address book

You will need:

4 pieces of fairly thick paper
20 x 30cm (8 x12in)
2 sheets of contrasting bright
paper 20 x 30cm (8 x 12in)
Thick bright paper 20 x 30cm
(8 x 12in) for the cover
A craft knife
A ruler and pencil
75cm (30in) of embroidery
thread and a large needle
Calligraphy pens
Glue and masking tape

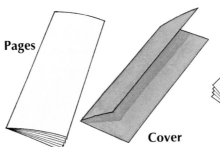

Pages

Cover

1. Fold the four sheets of thick paper in half. Place the pages inside each other to make a book. Score a line down the middle of the cover and fold it.

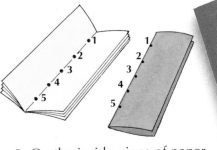

2. On the inside piece of paper make five light pencil marks at 5cm (2in) intervals along the fold. Do the same on the cover paper and number the marks.

3. Stitching the pages together

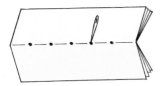

a) Push the needle through the pages at each mark on the fold.

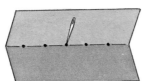

b) Do the same with the cardboard and put it around the pages.

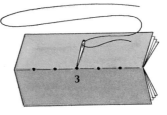

c) Thread the needle and push it through the book at hole 3.

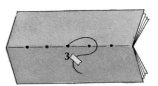

d) Leave about 20cm (8in) loose. Secure it with a little tape.

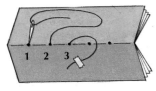

e) Push the needle up through hole 2 and down through 1.

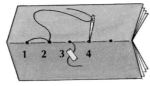

f) Stitch back up through 2 and down through 4.

g) Stitch up through 5, down through 4 and up through 3.

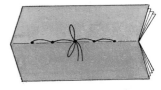

h) Tie the loose ends tightly in a double knot and trim the ends.

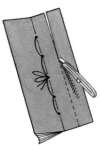
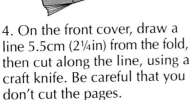

Fold back the back cover and pages so that you don't cut through them.

4. On the front cover, draw a line 5.5cm (2¼in) from the fold, then cut along the line, using a craft knife. Be careful that you don't cut the pages.

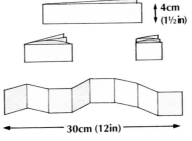

4cm (1½in)

30cm (12in)

5. Cut a strip of rough paper 30 x 4cm (12 x 1½in). Fold it in half three times to give eight equal sections. This will act as a guide for the decorated sections.

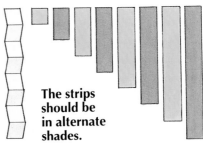

The strips should be in alternate shades.

6. Cut strips of bright paper 5 x 30 cm (2 x 12in). Using the guide, cut one section from one paper and two sections from the other, and so on.

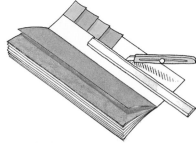

7. Stick the longest strip of bright paper onto the last page in the book. Stick the next longest onto the next page, and so on.

You could print a pattern on the cover with a rubber stamp (see pages 10-11), or cut out the word "ADDRESSES" from a contrasting shade and glue it on.

8. Fold back the cover and the rest of the pages in turn, so you can cut away the excess white paper at the bottom of each strip using a craft knife and a ruler.

Decorating the pages

Draw faint pencil lines at the bottom of each strip for the position of the letters. On rough paper, try out different styles of lettering to fill the spaces.

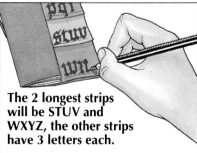

The 2 longest strips will be STUV and WXYZ, the other strips have 3 letters each.

Use a calligraphy pen to write the letters directly onto the strips, or use tracing paper to transfer your letters (see page 30), then fill them in.

A calligraphy nightshirt

You will need:

A large T-shirt
A large sheet of paper
Fabric paint from a craft shop
Clear book-covering film
A small sponge and a saucer
Masking tape and a craft knife
A large piece of cardboard
Paper towels
A ballpoint pen
A black felt-tip pen
A broad calligraphy pen

How to prepare your T-shirt

The cardboard stops the paint from soaking through to the back.

If the T-shirt is new, wash it to remove any 'finish'. Iron it to remove any creases. Slide the cardboard inside the T-shirt.

Masking tape   Paper towels

Place some paper towels between the front of the T-shirt and the cardboard. Smooth the fabric and secure it to the cardboard using masking tape.

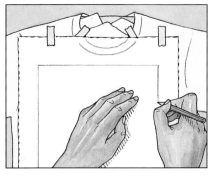

1. Spread the sheet of paper over the T-shirt and draw a rough outline of the area you want to decorate. Draw in the position of the arms and the neck.

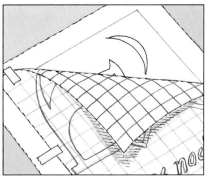

3. Outline your design with a black felt-tip pen. Tape a piece of book-covering film over the whole design, then draw over the lines with a ballpoint pen.

5. Peel the backing paper away from the film at the top. Stick it in place on the T-shirt. Gradually peel the rest of the backing away, sticking it down as you do it.

2. Place the paper onto a flat surface. Design your stencil inside the outline. Use double pencils (see page 3) or a calligraphy pen for the lettering.

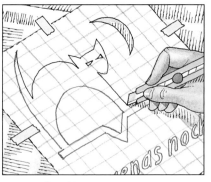

4. Put the film onto a cutting surface. Cut around each letter or shape and remove the pieces to leave a stencil. Keep any middle pieces of letters.

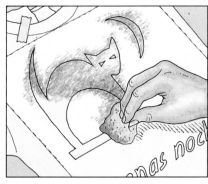

6. Pour some of the fabric paint onto a saucer. Dip the sponge into the paint and then gradually dab it all over the holes in your stencil to fill them in.

This T-shirt is decorated with small, intricate lettering. It is much easier to use large letters and simple shapes, as they are easier to cut out.

¡buenas noches!
Gute Nacht
ⲞⲞBRAHOC
GOOD NIGHT
bonne nuit

You could use the same method to print the name of a sport's team or club onto a T-shirt.

Draw a design to stencil onto boxer shorts or cycling shorts to wear with the nightshirt (see below right).

7. Leave the paint to dry thoroughly before peeling off the stencil. Follow the maker's instructions for 'fixing' the paint, so that the T-shirt can be washed.

Matching shorts

You could also decorate a pair of cycling shorts or boxer shorts in the same way as the T-shirt. Place the shorts onto a piece of paper and draw around them. Draw a design which fits onto the legs of the shorts. Follow the instructions from step 3.

A papier mâché bowl

Papier mâché takes quite a long time to do, but you do not need to do all the stages of sticking on the layers at one time. It also takes several days to dry out, but the results are worth waiting for.

You will need:

A large bowl
Newspaper cut into squares of about 4-5cm (1½-2in)
A small plastic container
Petroleum jelly
Artist's acrylic paints
PVA (household) glue
Emulsion paint
A thick and a fine paint brush
Carbon paper
Tracing paper
Masking tape
Self-adhesive labels
A sponge
A pair of scissors

1. Smear the inside of the bowl with an even layer of petroleum jelly to stop the newspaper from sticking to the bowl.

The tinted glue will help you to see each completed layer.

2. In a small container, mix six tablespoons of glue with two tablespoons of water. Tint the glue with a little acrylic paint.

Overlapping squares around the rim will be cut off later.

3. Lay squares of newspaper all over the greased surface of the bowl. Make sure they overlap each other slightly.

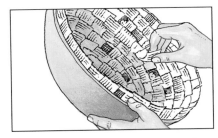

4. Paint the glue mixture gently over the surface and add another layer of squares. Overlap the rim of the bowl by about 3cm (1¼in).

Decorating the inside

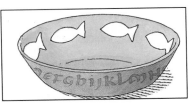

1. Cut out simple shapes from self-adhesive labels. Peel off the backing paper and stick them on at regular intervals.

2. Put some acrylic paint on a saucer. Press the sponge into it and dab the paint over the shapes and the inside.

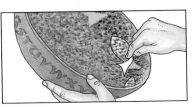

3. As soon as you have finished sponging on the paint, carefully remove the self-adhesive shapes.

4. Paint the inside of the bowl with two coats of the glue. Allow each coat to dry before painting on the next one.

Add extra layers on the base to stop the bowl from toppling over.

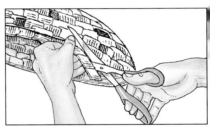

5. Add at least twelve more layers of glue and newspaper to make the bowl strong. Continue to overlap the rim with each layer.

6. Paint a final layer of glue on the inside of the bowl. Leave it in a warm place for two to three days to dry out completely.

7. Draw a line around the top of the original bowl, then ease out the papier mâché bowl and use scissors to cut around the line.

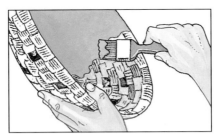

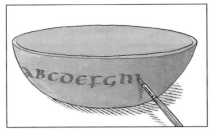

8. Stick squares over the rim to finish off the edge. Add a final layer of squares on the outside to make a smooth surface.

9. When dry, paint the inside of the bowl with emulsion paint, using the large brush. When this has dried, paint the outside.

10. Follow the instructions on page 15 to calculate the spacing of the letters on the outside of the bowl. Use acrylic paint for the lettering. Varnish with two coats of glue, allowing it to dry in between.

You cannot wash the bowl, but you can wipe it with a damp cloth to clean it.

Calligraphy and craft techniques

On these two pages you will find most of the techniques which are used in the projects.

Letter height

In each alphabet, the height of a letter is determined by the thickness of your pen nib. At the beginning of the alphabets on page 32, there is a small diagram showing you the number of nib widths the letters should be. This is called the x-height as it is the size of the small letter x in that alphabet. To find the x-height for the nib you are using, hold your pen nib at 90° and make small steps, one above the other.

An x-height of five nib widths.

The part which goes above the x-height is called an ascender.

This part is called a descender.

Measure guidelines using a ruler and a pencil so that the letters, ascenders and descenders are the same height.

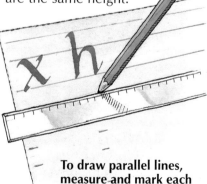

To draw parallel lines, measure and mark each point in at least two places and join the marks.

Spacing

Because letters are different shapes, the spaces between them cannot be measured exactly. Judge the spacing by eye so that it looks even. It's a good idea to try out your lettering on a piece of scrap paper before you work on any object. When you are happy with the spacing, trace over the lettering and transfer it to your object (see below).

Tracing

Once you have found the right spacing for your letters or words, trace around the outline of each letter with a pencil.

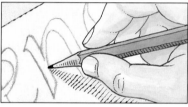

Scribble over the back of the lettering with a soft pencil, such as a B or 2B pencil.

Turn the tracing paper over and secure it in position with masking tape. Trace over the letters with a hard 2H pencil.

You can use carbon paper to transfer your lettering. This technique is described fully in the terracotta pot project (see pages 18-19). Dressmakers' carbon paper is best to use because it isn't inky or messy.

If you are using large lettering, draw each letter separately, cut them out and stick them in place.

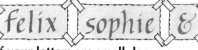

If your letters are small, leave a gap between each word the width of a letter 'o' in that alphabet.

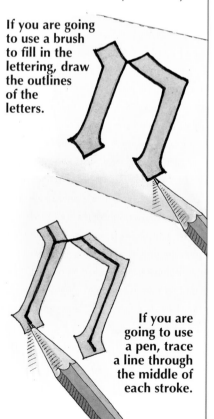

If you are going to use a brush to fill in the lettering, draw the outlines of the letters.

If you are going to use a pen, trace a line through the middle of each stroke.

Layout

The way lettering is arranged on an object is called layout. To place a word centrally, do the lettering on a rough piece of paper. Fold the paper in half to find the middle and trace or copy it onto your object.

Line up lettering to the left or right by cutting words into strips and taping them in position. Then, trace or copy them onto an object.

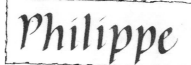

If the word is too long for a space, use a narrower nib and make the lettering smaller.

If a word doesn't fill a space, use a thicker nib and make the letters larger.

Folding paper and cardboard

Lightly fold the paper over, then run the bowl of a clean spoon along the fold to make a crease. To avoid marking your paper, place a piece of thin paper over the fold, then make the crease.

When folding cardboard or thick paper, it is best to score a line to fold along. Put a metal ruler along the line you wish to score, then run a craft knife along it very lightly. Do not cut into the cardboard or paper at all.

Using a craft knife

Always take special care when using a craft knife. Make a cutting surface using very thick cardboard or several old magazines to avoid cutting into the surface below. Try to cut away from the fingers which are holding the paper steady. When cutting a straight line, it is best to use a metal ruler.

When cutting thick cardboard, make several cuts in the same place, rather than trying to cut right through it.

When you have scored a line, fold the cardboard or paper along the line. It may help to hold a ruler along the scored line as you make the fold.

Calligraphy alphabets

Italic capital letters 45°

Nib width

A B C D E F G H I J K L M
N O P Q R S T U V W X Y Z

* Flatten nib to an angle of 20° for the 1st stroke of the letter A.

** Hold nib at 60° for the 1st stroke of N and the 1st and 3rd strokes of M.

*** Hold nib at an angle of 10°-15° for the capital and small italic Z.

Italic small letters 45°

a b c d e f g h i j k l m
n o p q r s t u v w x y z

Uncials 15°

a b c d e f g h i j k l m
n o p q r s t u v w x y z

* Hold nib at an angle of 0° for the letter Z.

Black letter or Gothic 40°

a b c d e f g h i j k l m
n o p q r s t u v w x y z

* Hold nib at an angle of 10°-15° for the letter Z.

Books to read

Calligraphy - Caroline Young (Usborne).
Teach Yourself Calligraphy - Patricia Lovett (Hodder and Stoughton).
Creating Letterforms - Rosemary Sassoon and Patricia Lovett (Thames and Hudson).
Creative Calligraphy - Rachel Yallop (Hodder and Stoughton).

Groups and societies

Ask in your local library for a list of calligraphy groups. 'Letters' is an international society for young people. It issues a newsletter which contains ideas and projects, and also runs workshops. Send a stamped addressed envelope to Letters, Hernewood, Gracious Lane, Sevenoaks, Kent. TN13 1TJ England for more information.

First published in 1994 by Usborne Publishing Ltd., Usborne House, 83-85 Saffron Hill, London EC1N 8RT, England. Copyright © 1994 Usborne Publishing Ltd. The name Usborne and the device are Trade Marks of Usborne Publishing Ltd. Printed in Portugal. First published in America in March 1995. UE.

CALLIGRAPHY PROJECTS

Fiona Watt and Anna Rowley

Designed by Rebecca Halverson

Illustrated by Jonathan Woodcock

Photographs by Amanda Heywood • Calligraphy by Patricia Lovett
Edited by Felicity Brooks

Contents

Starting out

The word calligraphy is used to describe any kind of beautiful lettering. It comes from two Greek words, *kalli* meaning "beauty" and *graphia* which means "to write". In this book you will find projects which use a variety of different calligraphy techniques.

Equipment

Before you start any of the projects, check that you have all the things you will need. You will probably have some of the equipment, but you may need to go to a craft shop or a stationer's to buy one or two items.

Letter styles

On page 32, you will find examples of calligraphy alphabets. The small numbers near to each letter indicate the order in which you make the pen strokes. The arrows show the direction of each stroke. Lift your pen off the paper between each stroke.

There is more information about spacing your letters and how to set out words on pages 30 -31. On these pages there are also details of some of the techniques used in the projects.

Start with line 1. Make the stroke in the direction of the arrow.

1

2

The second stroke also starts at the top.

Finally, add line 3 to complete the letter.

3

Pens and brushes

You will need a calligraphy pen for some of the projects. There are many different types which you can buy, but the easiest to use are calligraphy felt-tip pens. They are suitable for most of the projects in this book. They have broad, square ends and come in a variety of widths and shades.

You can also buy special metal-nibbed, calligraphy 'dip' pens or fountain pens which you fill with ink or paint. They come with nibs of different widths and produce sharper lines than felt-tip pens. To find out how to use one, follow the maker's instructions, or look in the books listed on page 32. Broad-edge brushes, also known as one-stroke brushes, can be bought at an art supplier's.

Drawing inks

This picture shows a variety of equipment which can be used for decorating paper and objects with calligraphy.

Felt-tip pen

Calligraphy felt-tip pen

Calligraphy gold felt-tip pen

Broad-edge (one-stroke) brush

A calligraphy fountain pen

A tube of gouache paint

Nib angles

Writing with a broad-edged nib gives you a variety of thick and thin lines. The shape of the letter depends on the angle at which you hold the nib. For most alphabets, the nib should be held at the same angle throughout. The angle is shown by a diagram at the beginning of each alphabet (see page 32).

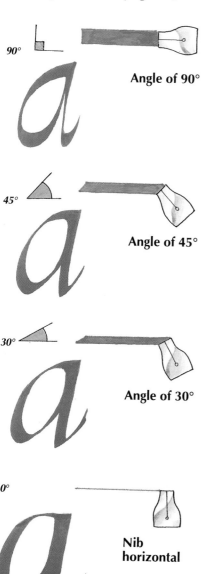

90°

Angle of 90°

45°

Angle of 45°

30°

Angle of 30°

0°

Nib horizontal

Double pencils

To get used to making smooth letter strokes with a calligraphy pen or brush, try taping two pencils together with masking tape. If you are right-handed, place the paper you are working on straight in front of you. If you are left-handed, you may find it easier to place the paper at an angle of about 45° on your work surface (see box below).

Tape two flat-sided pencils together with some masking tape.

If you are left-handed, tape one pencil about 5mm (²/₁₀ in) lower than the other one.

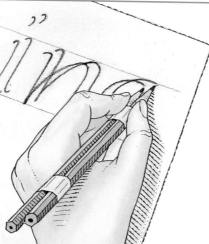

Left-handers

If you are left-handed, use a pen with a left-oblique nib or double pencils taped as shown above. You may need to change the angle of your wrist or the way you hold the pencils or pen, so that your wrist is under your lettering. Also, try placing your paper at an angle of 45° on your work surface.

If you haven't tried any calligraphy before, try making simple letter strokes with your double pencils.

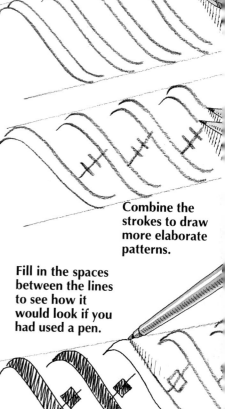

Combine the strokes to draw more elaborate patterns.

Fill in the spaces between the lines to see how it would look if you had used a pen.

Embossed notepaper

Embossing is the shaping or carving of letters or patterns so that they are raised above the surrounding surface.

You will need:

Writing paper and an envelope with a V-shaped flap
2 pieces of thin cardboard the same size as the writing paper
A craft knife
A teaspoon
Double pencils (see page 3)
Paper clips and glue
A fine felt-tip pen

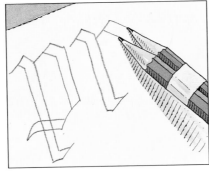

1. Using double pencils draw your initials on one piece of cardboard. Draw them in the same position as you want them to be on your writing paper.

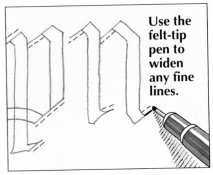

Use the felt-tip pen to widen any fine lines.

2. Make any thin parts of letters about 2mm ($^1/_{16}$in) wide, then put some old magazines under the cardboard to protect your work surface.

Keep any cut-out middle pieces of letters.

3. Cut out each letter with the craft knife. Then turn the cardboard over and glue it onto the other piece of cardboard. Glue any middle pieces in place.

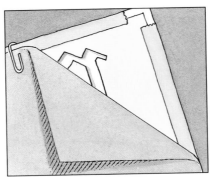

4. Place a sheet of writing paper over the cardboard. Secure it in place with some paper clips. Lay the paper and cardboard on a flat surface.

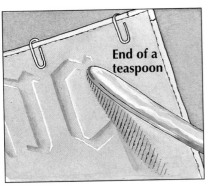

End of a teaspoon

5. Gently push the paper into the cut-out letters, using the end of the spoon. Push right into the edges of the letters to make crisp lines.

6. Carefully remove the paper clips and turn the paper over. You can make many sheets of embossed paper using the same cardboard cut-out.